JAZZ PLAY ALONG®

Book and CD for B♭, E♭ and C Instruments

VOLUME 61

Arranged and Produced by Mark Taylor, Jim Roberts & Paul Murtha

MONGO SANTAMARIA

Jazz Favorites

BOOK

CD

Cover Photo by "PoPsie" Randolph

ISBN-13: 978-1-4234-1339-4
ISBN-10: 1-4234-1339-3

HAL•LEONARD® CORPORATION

7777 W. BLUEMOUND RD. P.O. BOX 13819 MILWAUKEE, WI 53213

Visit Hal Leonard Online at
www.halleonard.com

Mongo Santamaria

HAL•LEONARD
JAZZ PLAY ALONG®

Volume 61

Arranged and Produced by
Mark Taylor, Jim Roberts & Paul Murtha

Featured Players:

Graham Breedlove–Trumpet
John Desalme–Saxophones
Tony Nalker–Piano
Jim Roberts–Bass
Steve Fidyk–Drums

Recorded at Bias Studios, Springfield, Virginia
Bob Dawson, Engineer

HOW TO USE THE CD:

Each song has <u>two</u> tracks:

1) Split Track/Melody

Woodwind, Brass, Keyboard, and **Mallet Players** can use this track as a learning tool for melody style and inflection.

Bass Players can learn and perform with this track – remove the recorded bass track by turning down the volume on the LEFT channel.

Keyboard and **Guitar Players** can learn and perform with this track – remove the recorded piano part by turning down the volume on the RIGHT channel.

2) Full Stereo Track

Soloists or **Groups** can learn and perform with this accompaniment track with the RHYTHM SECTION only.

AFRO BLUE

BY MONGO SANTAMARIA

C VERSION

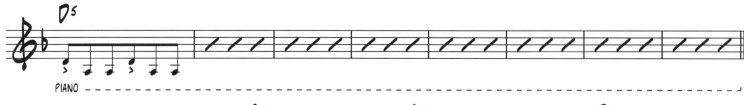

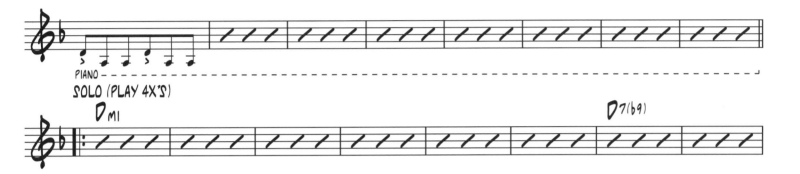

SOLO (PLAY 4X'S)

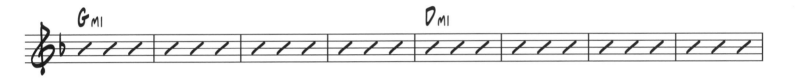

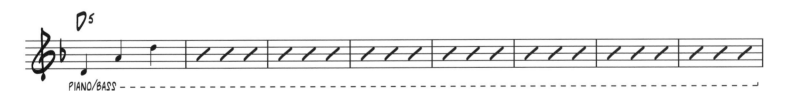

PLAY

COME CANDELLIA

BY MONGO SANTAMARIA

C VERSION

LAS GUAJIRAS

BY MONGO SANTAMARIA

CD

7 : SPLIT TRACK/MELODY
8 : FULL STEREO TRACK

C VERSION

FEDERICO

BY MONGO SANTAMARIA

C VERSION

SOLO (15 CHORUSES)

LAST X ONLY

LINDA GUAJIRA

BY MONGO SANTAMARIA

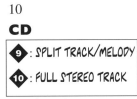

CD

9 : SPLIT TRACK/MELODY
10 : FULL STEREO TRACK

C VERSION

MED. LATIN

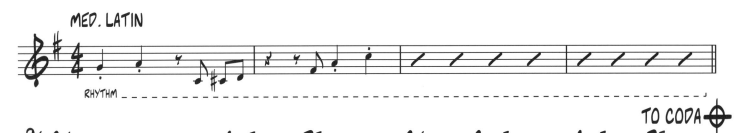

PARA TI

BY MONGO SANTAMARIA

CD
13 : SPLIT TRACK/MELODY
14 : FULL STEREO TRACK

C VERSION

MEDIUM LATIN

SOLO BREAK (PLAY 6X'S)

SOLOS (PLAY 24X'S)

CD

11 : SPLIT TRACK/MELODY
12 : FULL STEREO TRACK

MANILA

BY MONGO SANTAMARIA

C VERSION

CD
◆15: SPLIT TRACK/MELODY
◆16: FULL STEREO TRACK

PAY JUAQUIN

BY MONGO SANTAMARIA

C VERSION

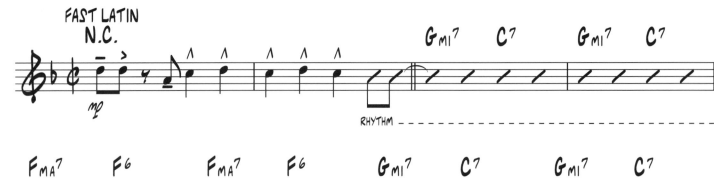

CD

17 : SPLIT TRACK/MELODY
18 : FULL STEREO TRACK

C VERSION

SABROSO

BY MONGO SANTAMARIA

A⁷   D⁶   A⁷   D⁶

A⁷   D⁶   A⁷   D⁶

SOLOS (PLAY 14X'S)

A⁷   D⁶   A⁷   D⁶

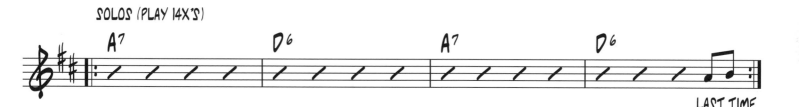

LAST TIME

N.C.

WATERMELON MAN

CD
◆19: SPLIT TRACK/MELODY
◆20: FULL STEREO TRACK

BY HERBIE HANCOCK

C VERSION

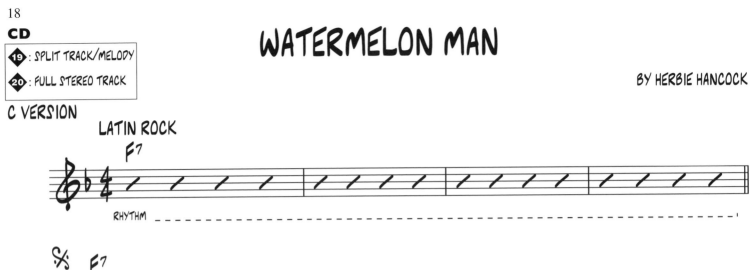

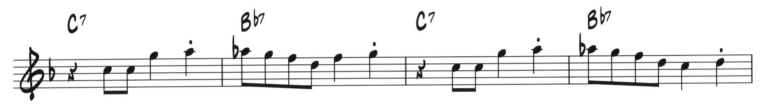

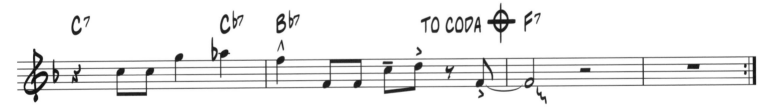

COME CANDELLIA

BY MONGO SANTAMARIA

Bb VERSION

MEDIUM LATIN

AFRO BLUE

BY MONGO SANTAMARIA

Bb VERSION

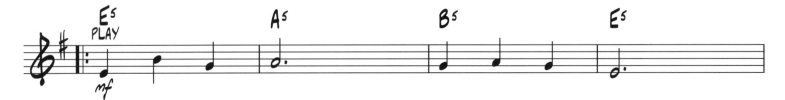

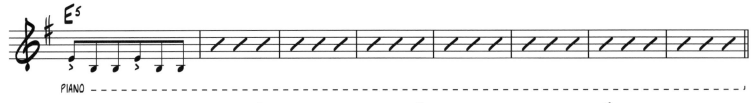

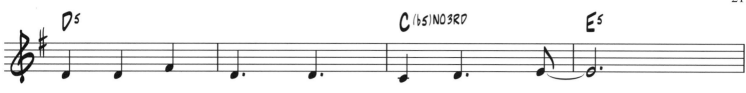

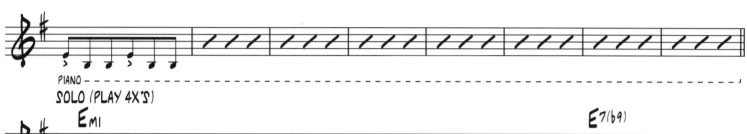

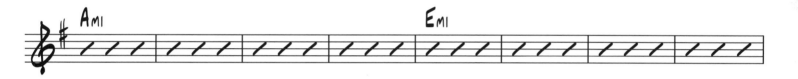

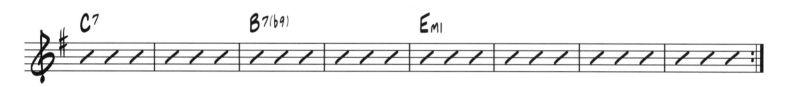

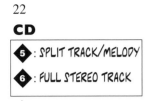

FEDERICO

BY MONGO SANTAMARIA

B♭ VERSION

SOLO (15 CHORUSES)

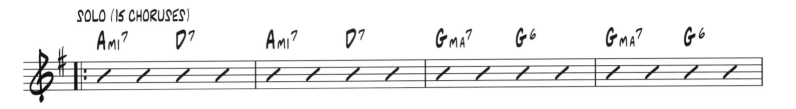

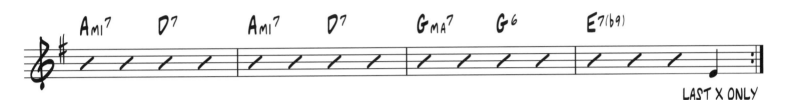

LAST X ONLY

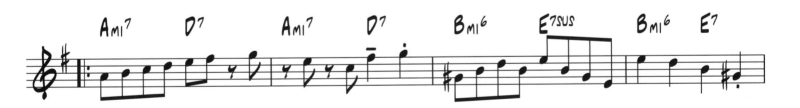

LAS GUAJIRAS

BY MONGO SANTAMARIA

LINDA GUAJIRA

BY MONGO SANTAMARIA

MANILA

BY MONGO SANTAMARIA

CD

13 : SPLIT TRACK/MELODY
14 : FULL STEREO TRACK

PARA TI

BY MONGO SANTAMARIA

B♭ VERSION

MEDIUM LATIN

SOLO BREAK (PLAY 6X'S)

SOLOS (PLAY 24X'S)

N.C.

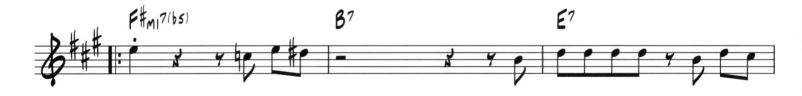

WATERMELON MAN

BY HERBIE HANCOCK

Bb VERSION

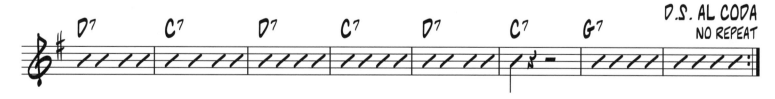

PAY JUAQUIN

BY MONGO SANTAMARIA

Bb VERSION

FAST LATIN

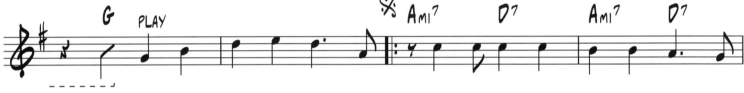

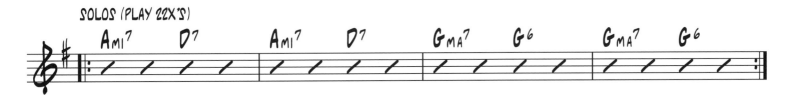

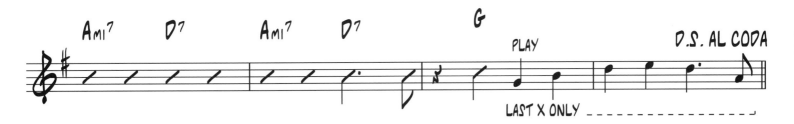

SABROSO

BY MONGO SANTAMARIA

Bb VERSION

SOLOS (PLAY 14X'S)

LAST TIME

AFRO BLUE

BY MONGO SANTAMARIA

E♭ VERSION

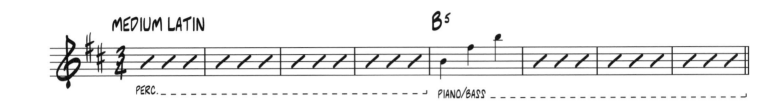

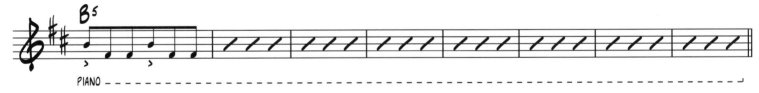

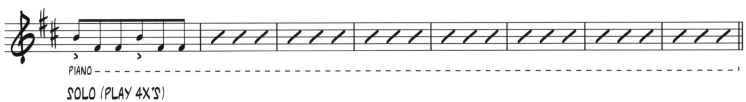

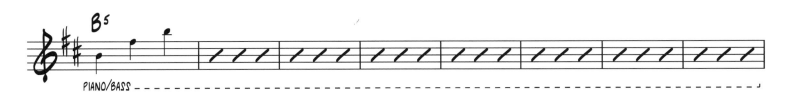

CD
3 : SPLIT TRACK/MELODY
4 : FULL STEREO TRACK

COME CANDELLIA

BY MONGO SANTAMARIA

E♭ VERSION

LAS GUAJIRAS

BY MONGO SANTAMARIA

FEDERICO

BY MONGO SANTAMARIA

E♭ VERSION

FAST LATIN

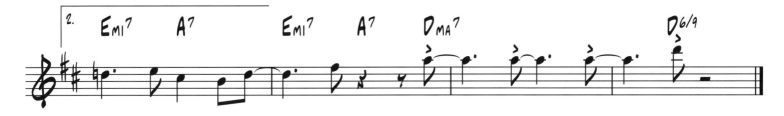

LINDA GUAJIRA

BY MONGO SANTAMARIA

CD
- **9**: SPLIT TRACK/MELODY
- **10**: FULL STEREO TRACK

E♭ VERSION

MED. LATIN

RHYTHM _ _ _ _ _ _ _ _

TO CODA ⊕

N.C.

RHYTHM _ _ _ _ _ _

PLAY

SOLO (PLAY 20X'S)

LAST TIME

D.S. AL CODA
TAKE REPEAT

⊕ CODA
N.C.

PARA TI

BY MONGO SANTAMARIA

E♭ VERSION

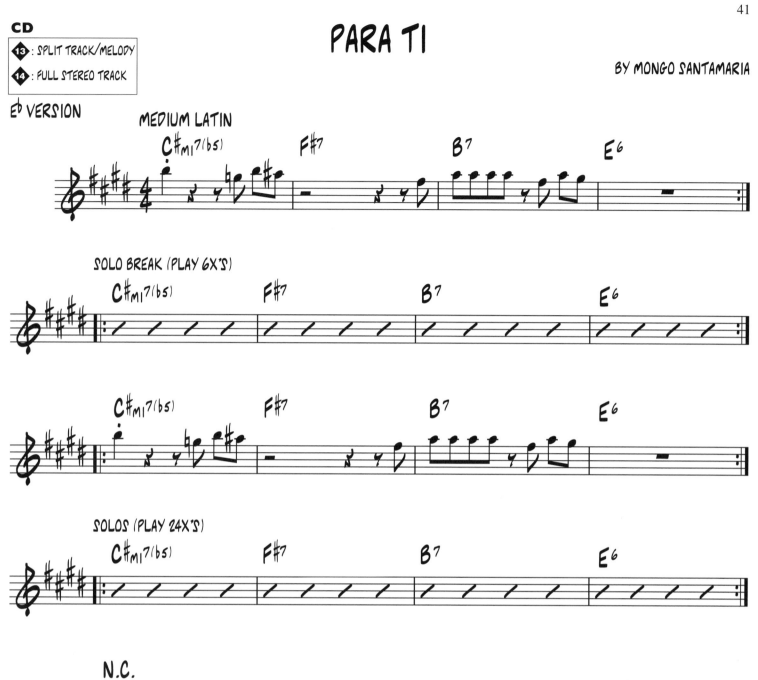

MANILA

BY MONGO SANTAMARIA

PAY JUAQUIN

BY MONGO SANTAMARIA

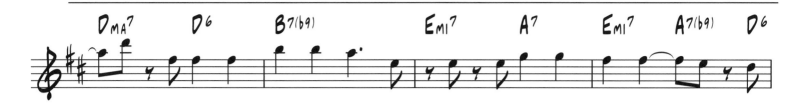

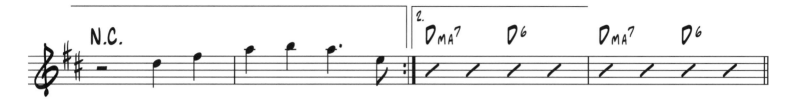

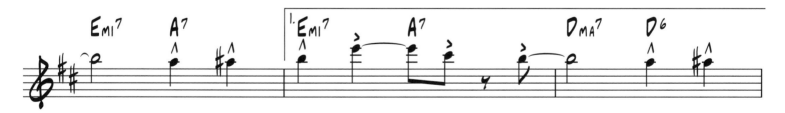

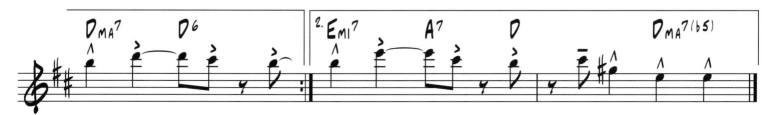

Eb VERSION

SABROSO

BY MONGO SANTAMARIA

SOLOS (PLAY 14X'S)

LAST TIME

N.C.

CD
19: SPLIT TRACK/MELODY
20: FULL STEREO TRACK

WATERMELON MAN

BY HERBIE HANCOCK

E♭ VERSION

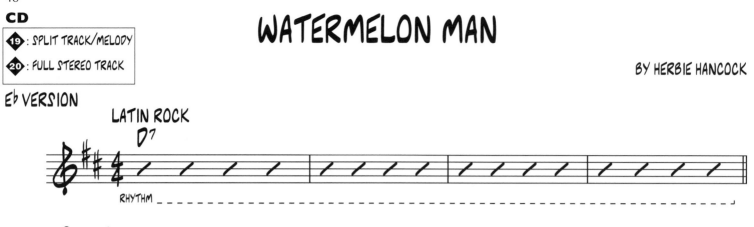

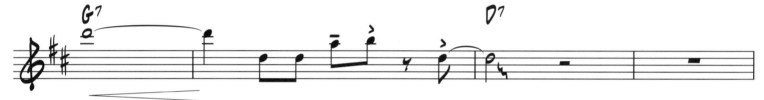

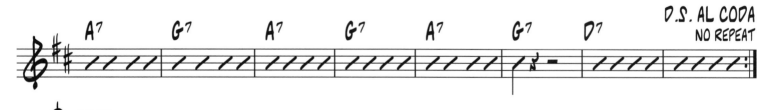

COME CANDELLIA

BY MONGO SANTAMARIA

: SPLIT TRACK/MELODY
: FULL STEREO TRACK

♪: C VERSION   MEDIUM LATIN

AFRO BLUE

CD

❶: SPLIT TRACK/MELODY
❷: FULL STEREO TRACK

BY MONGO SANTAMARIA

C VERSION

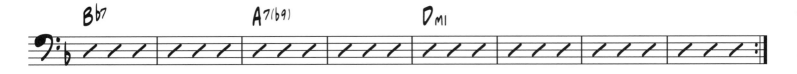

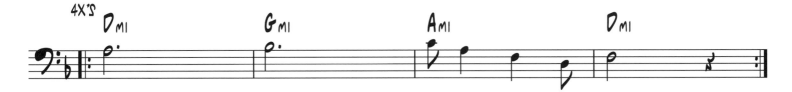

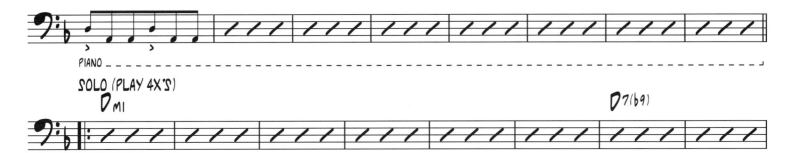

FEDERICO

BY MONGO SANTAMARIA

♪: C VERSION

FAST LATIN

CD

7 : SPLIT TRACK/MELODY
8 : FULL STEREO TRACK

LAS GUAJIRAS

BY MONGO SANTAMARIA

C VERSION   MEDIUM LATIN

LINDA GUAJIRA

BY MONGO SANTAMARIA

MANILA

BY MONGO SANTAMARIA

PARA TI

BY MONGO SANTAMARIA

WATERMELON MAN

BY HERBIE HANCOCK

CD

15 : SPLIT TRACK/MELODY
16 : FULL STEREO TRACK

PAY JUAQUIN

BY MONGO SANTAMARIA

𝄢: C VERSION

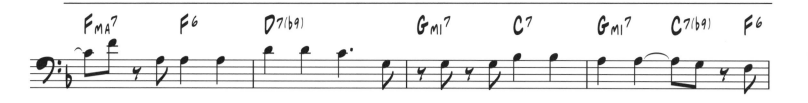

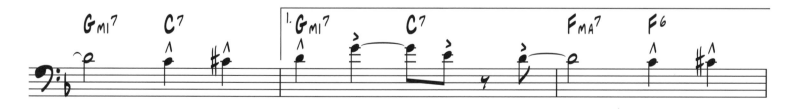

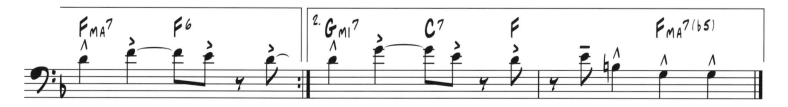

SABROSO

BY MONGO SANTAMARIA

CD
17 : SPLIT TRACK/MELODY
18 : FULL STEREO TRACK

𝄢: C VERSION

SOLOS (PLAY 14X'S)

LAST TIME

N.C.

  **Presenting the Hal Leonard** JAZZ PLAY ALONG SERIES

DUKE ELLINGTON Vol. 1 00841644
Caravan • Don't Get Around Much Anymore • In a Sentimental Mood • Perdido • Prelude to a Kiss • Satin Doll • Take the "A" Train • and more.

MILES DAVIS Vol. 2 00841645
All Blues • Blue in Green • Four • Half Nelson • Milestones • Nardis • Seven Steps to Heaven • So What • Solar • Tune Up.

THE BLUES Vol. 3 00841646
Billie's Bounce • Birk's Works • C-Jam Blues • Freddie Freeloader • Mr. P.C. • Tenor Madness • Things Ain't What They Used to Be • and more.

JAZZ BALLADS Vol. 4 00841691
Body and Soul • Here's That Rainy Day • Misty • My Funny Valentine • The Nearness of You • Polka Dots and Moonbeams • and more.

BEST OF BEBOP Vol. 5 00841689
Anthropology • Donna Lee • Doxy • Epistrophy • Lady Bird • Oleo • Ornithology • Scrapple from the Apple • Woodyn' You • Yardbird Suite.

JAZZ CLASSICS WITH EASY CHANGES Vol. 6 00841690
Blue Train • Comin' Home Baby • Footprints • Impressions • Killer Joe • St. Thomas • Well You Needn't • and more.

ESSENTIAL JAZZ STANDARDS Vol. 7 00843000
Autumn Leaves • Lullaby of Birdland • Stella by Starlight • There Will Never Be Another You • When Sunny Gets Blue • and more.

ANTONIO CARLOS JOBIM AND THE ART OF THE BOSSA NOVA Vol. 8 00843001
The Girl from Ipanema • How Insensitive • Meditation • One Note Samba • Quiet Nights of Quiet Stars • Slightly Out of Tune • and more.

DIZZY GILLESPIE Vol. 9 00843002
Birk's Works • Con Alma • Groovin' High • Manteca • A Night in Tunisia • Salt Peanuts • Tour De Force • Woodyn' You • and more.

DISNEY CLASSICS Vol. 10 00843003
Alice in Wonderland • Cruella De Vil • When You Wish upon a Star • You've Got a Friend in Me • Zip-a-Dee-Doo-Dah • and more.

RODGERS AND HART FAVORITES Vol. 11 00843004
Bewitched • Dancing on the Ceiling • Have You Met Miss Jones? • I Could Write a Book • The Lady Is a Tramp • My Romance • and more.

ESSENTIAL JAZZ CLASSICS Vol. 12 00843005
Airegin • Ceora • The Frim Fram Sauce • Israel • Milestones • Nefertiti • Red Clay • Satin Doll • Song for My Father • Take Five.

JOHN COLTRANE Vol. 13 00843006
Blue Train • Countdown • Cousin Mary • Equinox • Giant Steps • Impressions • Lazy Bird • Mr. P.C. • Moment's Notice • Naima.

IRVING BERLIN Vol. 14 00843007
Blue Skies • How Deep Is the Ocean • I've Got My Love to Keep Me Warm • Steppin' Out with My Baby • What'll I Do? • and more.

RODGERS & HAMMERSTEIN Vol. 15 00843008
Do I Love You Because You're Beautiful? • It Might as Well Be Spring • My Favorite Things • Younger Than Springtime • and more.

COLE PORTER Vol. 16 00843009
Easy to Love • I Concentrate on You • I've Got You Under My Skin • It's All Right with Me • It's De-Lovely • You'd Be So Nice to Come Home To • and more.

COUNT BASIE Vol. 17 00843010
All of Me • April in Paris • Blues in Hoss Flat • Li'l Darlin' • Moten Swing • One O'Clock Jump • Shiny Stockings • Until I Met You • and more.

HAROLD ARLEN Vol. 18 00843011
Ac-cent-tchu-ate the Positive • Come Rain or Come Shine • I've Got the World on a String • Stormy Weather • That Old Black Magic • and more.

COOL JAZZ Vol. 19 00843012
Bernie's Tune • Boplicity • Budo • Conception • Django • Five Brothers • Line for Lyons • Walkin' Shoes • Waltz for Debby • Whisper Not.

RODGERS AND HART CLASSICS Vol. 21 00843014
Falling in Love with Love • Isn't it Romantic? • Manhattan • My Funny Valentine • This Can't Be Love • Thou Swell • Where or When • and more.

WAYNE SHORTER Vol. 22 00843015
Children of the Night • ESP • Footprints • Juju • Mahjong • Nefertiti • Nightdreamer • Speak No Evil • Witch Hunt • Yes and No.

LATIN JAZZ Vol. 23 00843016
Agua De Beber • Chega De Saudade • Manha De Carnaval • Mas Que Nada • Ran Kan Kan • So Nice • Watch What Happens • and more.

EARLY JAZZ STANDARDS Vol. 24 00843017
After You've Gone • Avalon • Indian Summer • Indiana • Ja-Da • Limehouse Blues • Paper Doll • Poor Butterfly • Rose Room • St. Louis Blues.

CHRISTMAS JAZZ Vol. 25 00843018
The Christmas Song (Chestnuts Roasting on an Open Fire) • I'll Be Home for Christmas • Let It Snow! Let It Snow! Let It Snow! • Silver Bells • and more.

CHARLIE PARKER Vol. 26 00843019
Au Privave • Billie's Bounce • Donna Lee • My Little Suede Shoes • Ornithology • Scrapple from the Apple • Yardbird Suite • and more.

GREAT JAZZ STANDARDS Vol. 27 00843020
Fly Me to the Moon • How High the Moon • I Can't Get Started with You • Speak Low • Tangerine • Willow Weep for Me • and more.

BIG BAND ERA Vol. 28 00843021
Air Mail Special • Christopher Columbus • In the Mood • Jersey Bounce • Opus One • Stompin' at the Savoy • Tuxedo Junction • and more.

LENNON AND MCCARTNEY Vol. 29 00843022
And I Love Her • Blackbird • Come Together • Eleanor Rigby • Let It Be • Ticket to Ride • Yesterday • and more.

BLUES' BEST Vol. 30 00843023
Basin Street Blues • Bloomdido • Happy Go Lucky Local • K.C. Blues • Sonnymoon for Two • Take the Coltrane • Turnaround • Twisted • and more.

JAZZ IN THREE Vol. 31 00843024
Bluesette • Jitterbug Waltz • Moon River • Tennessee Waltz • West Coast Blues • What the World Needs Now Is Love • Wives and Lovers • and more.

BEST OF SWING Vol. 32 00843025
Alright, Okay, You Win • Cherokee • I'll Be Seeing You • Jump, Jive An' Wail • On the Sunny Side of the Street • Route 66 • Sentimental Journey • and more.

SONNY ROLLINS Vol. 33 00843029
Airegin • Alfie's Theme • Biji • The Bridge • Doxy • First Moves • Here's to the People • Oleo • St. Thomas • Sonnymoon for Two.

ALL TIME STANDARDS Vol. 34 00843030
Autumn in New York • Bye Bye Blackbird • Call Me Irresponsible • Georgia on My Mind • Honeysuckle Rose • Stardust • The Very Thought of You • more.

BLUESY JAZZ Vol. 35 00843031
Angel Eyes • Bags' Groove • Bessie's Blues • Chitlins Con Carne • Mercy, Mercy, Mercy • Night Train • Sweet Georgia Bright • and more.

HORACE SILVER Vol. 36 00843032
Doodlin' • The Jody Grind • Nica's Dream • Opus De Funk • Peace • The Preacher • Senor Blues • Sister Sadie • Song for My Father • Strollin'.

BILL EVANS Vol. 37 00843033 ($16.95)
Funkallero • My Bells • One for Helen • The Opener • Orbit • Show-Type Tune • 34 Skidoo • Time Remembered • Turn Out the Stars • Waltz for Debby.

YULETIDE JAZZ Vol. 38 00843034
Blue Christmas • Christmas Time Is Here • Merry Christmas, Darling • The Most Wonderful Time of the Year • Santa Claus Is Comin' to Town • and more.

"ALL THE THINGS YOU ARE" & MORE JEROME KERN SONGS Vol. 39 00843035
All the Things You Are • Can't Help Lovin' Dat Man • A Fine Romance • Long Ago (And Far Away) • The Way You Look Tonight • Yesterdays • and more.

BOSSA NOVA Vol. 40 00843036
Black Orpheus • Call Me • A Man and a Woman • Only Trust Your Heart • The Shadow of Your Smile • Watch What Happens • Wave • and more.

CLASSIC DUKE ELLINGTON Vol. 41 00843037
Cotton Tail • Do Nothin' Till You Hear from Me • I Got It Bad and That Ain't Good • I'm Beginning to See the Light • Mood Indigo • Solitude • and more.

GERRY MULLIGAN CLASSICS Vol. 43 00843039
Apple Core • Line for Lyons • Nights at the Turntable • Song for Strayhorn • Walkin' Shoes • and more.

OLIVER NELSON Vol. 44 00843040
The Drive • Emancipation Blues • Hoe-Down • I Remember Bird • Miss Fine • Stolen Moments • Straight Ahead • Teenie's Blues • Yearnin'.

JAZZ AT THE MOVIES Vol. 45 00843041
Baby Elephant Walk • God Bless' the Child • The Look of Love • The Rainbow Connection • Swinging on a Star • Thanks for the Memory • and more.

BROADWAY JAZZ STANDARDS Vol. 46 00843042
Ain't Misbehavin' • I've Grown Accustomed to Her Face • Make Someone Happy • Old Devil Moon • Small World • Till There Was You • and more.

CLASSIC JAZZ BALLADS Vol. 47 00843043
Blame It on My Youth • It's Easy to Remember • June in January • Love Letters • A Nightingale Sang in Berkeley Square • When I Fall in Love • and more.

BEBOP CLASSICS Vol. 48 00843044
Be-Bop • Bird Feathers • Blue 'N Boogie • Byrd Like • Cool Blues • Dance of the Indifels • Dexterity • Dizzy Atmosphere • Groovin' High • Tempus Fugit.

MILES DAVIS STANDARDS Vol. 49 00843045
Darn That Dream • I Loves You, Porgy • If I Were a Bell • On Green Dolphin Street • Some Day My Prince Will Come • Yesterdays • and more.

GREAT JAZZ CLASSICS Vol. 50 00843046
Along Came Betty • Birdland • The Jive Samba • Little Sunflower • Nuages • Peri's Scope • Phase Dance • Road Song • Think on Me • Windows.

UP-TEMPO JAZZ Vol. 51 00843047
Cherokee (Indian Love Song) • Chi Chi • 52nd Street Theme • Little Willie Leaps • Move • Pent Up House • Topsy • and more.

STEVIE WONDER Vol. 52 00843048
I Just Called to Say I Love You • Isn't She Lovely • My Cherie Amour • Part Time Lover • Superstition • You Are the Sunshine of My Life • and more.

RHYTHM CHANGES Vol. 53 00843049
Celia • Chasing the Bird • Cotton Tail • Crazeology • Fox Hunt • I Got Rhythm • No Moe • Oleo • Red Cross • Steeplechase.

"MOONLIGHT IN VERMONT" AND OTHER GREAT STANDARDS Vol. 54 00843050
A Child Is Born • Love You Madly • Lover Man (Oh, Where Can You Be?) • Moonlight in Vermont • The Night Has a Thousand Eyes • Small Fry • and more.

BENNY GOLSON Vol. 55 00843052
Along Came Betty • Blues March • Gypsy Jingle-Jangle • I Remember Clifford • Killer Joe • Step Lightly • Whisper Not • and more.